Scary Creatures
DINOSAURS

Written by
John Cooper

Illustrated by
Mark Bergin and
Carolyn Scrace

W
FRANKLIN WATTS
A Division of Scholastic Inc.
NEW YORK • TORONTO • LONDON • AUCKLAND • SYDNEY
MEXICO CITY • NEW DELHI • HONG KONG
DANBURY, CONNECTICUT

Created and designed by
David Salariya

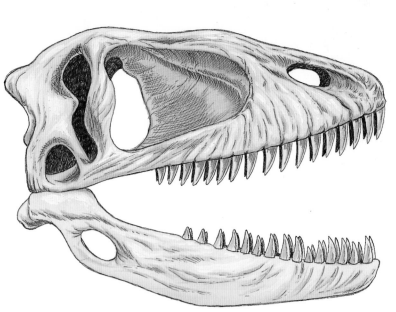

Author:

John Cooper is a geologist and Keeper of the Booth Museum of Natural History in Brighton, England. He has studied dinosaurs in Leicestershire and Sussex, England and at the Carnegie Museum of Natural History in Pittsburgh, Pennsylvania. He is the author of several books on dinosaurs and related subjects.

Artists:

Mark Bergin was born in Hastings, England, in 1961. He studied at Eastbourne College of Art and has illustrated many children's non-fiction books. He lives in Bexhill-on-Sea, England, with his wife and three children.

Carolyn Scrace is a graduate of Brighton College of Art, England, specializing in design and illustration. She has worked in animation, advertising, and children's fiction and non-fiction, particularly natural history.

Additional Artist:
Nick Hewetson

Series Creator:

David Salariya was born in Dundee, Scotland. In 1989, he established The Salariya Book Company. He has illustrated a wide range of books and has created many new series for publishers in the U.K. and overseas. He lives in Brighton, England, with his wife, illustrator Shirley Willis, and their son.

Editors:

Stephanie Cole
Karen Barker Smith

Photo Credits:

Daniel Heuclin, NHPA: 12
The Natural History Museum, London: 8, 11, 16/17, 26, 27
Kevin Schafer, NHPA: 25
Tom & Therisa Stack, NHPA: 20

Created, designed, and produced by
The Salariya Book Company Ltd
Book House,
25 Marlborough Place,
Brighton BN1 1UB

Visit the Salariya Book Company at
www.salariya.com

A CIP catalog record for this title is available from the Library of Congress.

ISBN 978-0-531-14669-9 (Lib. Bdg.)
ISBN 978-0-531-14851-8 (Pbk.)

Published in the United States by Franklin Watts
A Division of Scholastic Inc.
90 Sherman Turnpike
Danbury, CT 06816

Printed in China.
Printed on paper from sustainable forests.
Reprinted in 2009.

Contents

What Is a Dinosaur?

Dinosaurs were one of several types of **reptiles** which lived long ago. For millions of years they lived almost everywhere around the world, but they disappeared 65 million years ago. Dinosaurs lived on the land. They had strong legs and were good walkers or runners. Many were huge but some were small.

Lizards are not dinosaurs, although they are reptiles and just as old. Lizards are small and very fast. They can also be fierce. Unlike dinosaurs, the legs of lizards stick out sideways from their body and could never carry the weight of a larger creature. Dinosaurs legs were positioned directly beneath the body.

Is a lizard a dinosaur?

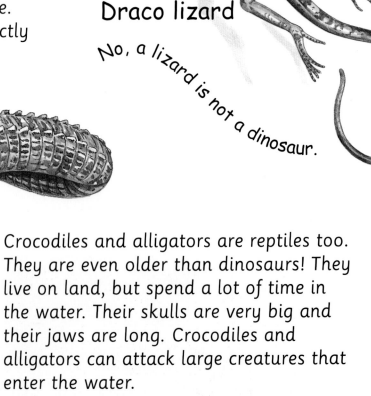

Draco lizard

No, a lizard is not a dinosaur.

Is a crocodile a dinosaur?

No, a crocodile is not a dinosaur.

Crocodiles and alligators are reptiles too. They are even older than dinosaurs! They live on land, but spend a lot of time in the water. Their skulls are very big and their jaws are long. Crocodiles and alligators can attack large creatures that enter the water.

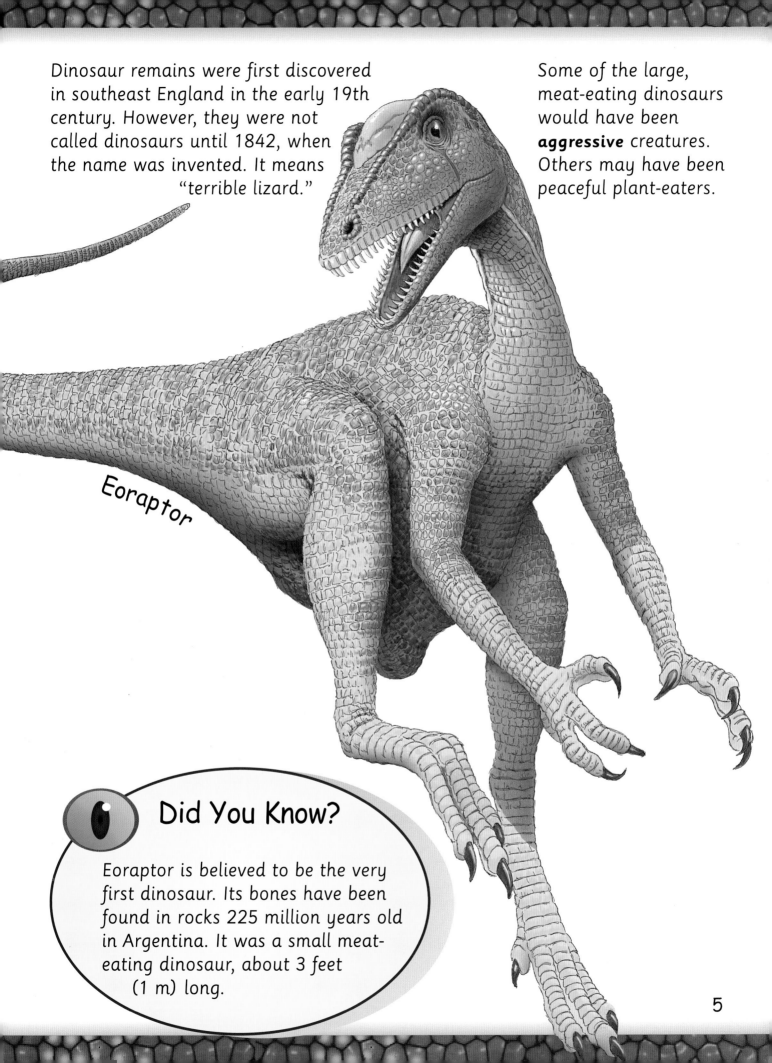

Dinosaur remains were first discovered in southeast England in the early 19th century. However, they were not called dinosaurs until 1842, when the name was invented. It means "terrible lizard."

Some of the large, meat-eating dinosaurs would have been **aggressive** creatures. Others may have been peaceful plant-eaters.

Eoraptor

Did You Know?

Eoraptor is believed to be the very first dinosaur. Its bones have been found in rocks 225 million years old in Argentina. It was a small meat-eating dinosaur, about 3 feet (1 m) long.

How Long Ago Did Dinosaurs Live?

Dinosaurs lived between 225 and 65 million years ago. They lived on Earth for 160 million years! The dinosaurs were not the first reptiles. Many different types of small lizards lived before them. Some of these reptiles survived to live alongside the dinosaurs. Some, such as lizards and crocodiles, still live today.

What did Earth look like millions of years ago?

Dinosaurs lived so long ago that it is impossible to imagine the passing of so much time. In all those millions of years the continents, seas, oceans, and weather have all changed.

It would be difficult for us to recognize Earth 200 million years ago. The plants and animals were very different then. We might be able to recognize some of them, but others are **extinct** now.

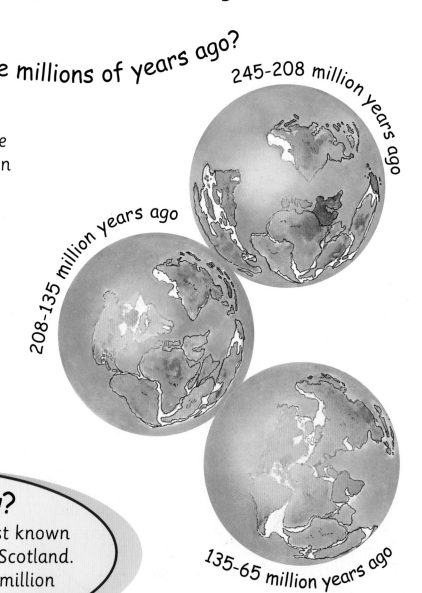

245-208 million years ago

208-135 million years ago

135-65 million years ago

Did You Know?

Remains of the earliest known reptile were found in Scotland. This reptile lived 335 million years ago.

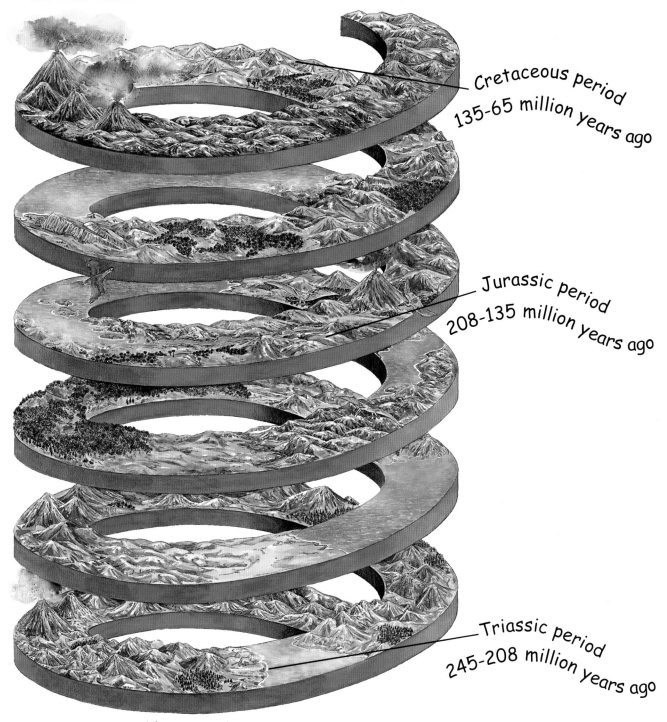

Cretaceous period
135-65 million years ago

Jurassic period
208-135 million years ago

Triassic period
245-208 million years ago

Mesozoic era

The dinosaurs lived in a time known as the Mesozoic era, meaning "middle life." This spiral represents the Mesozoic era. The oldest known dinosaur **fossils** were found in rocks that are about 225 million years old. These rocks are from a period of time called the **Triassic**. Scientists believe that most dinosaurs lived in the **Jurassic** period. Fewer dinosaurs lived in the **Cretaceous** period than the Triassic and Jurassic periods. By the end of the Cretaceous period the dinosaurs were extinct.

7

What Did Dinosaurs Eat?

Like most creatures alive today, dinosaurs ate either meat or plants. Meat-eating animals are called **carnivores**. Plant-eating animals are **herbivores**. Some animals eat both meat and plants. These animals are called omnivores. Many of the dinosaurs were herbivores.

Herbivores have rows of teeth which help grind plant leaves and stems before swallowing. Herbivores are attacked by meat-eaters, so they often have horns for protection, like this Triceratops (below).

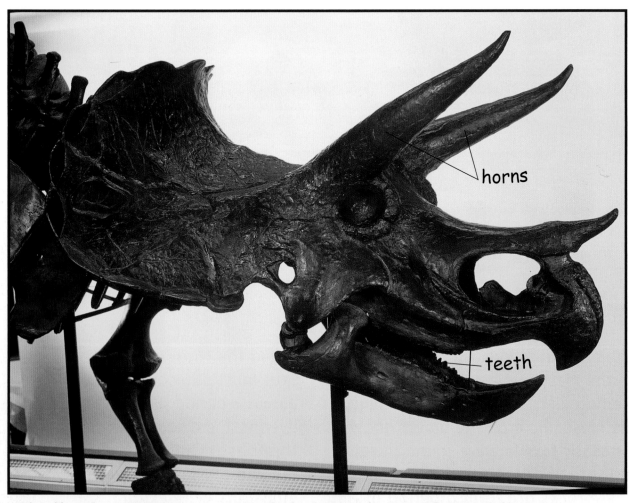

horns

teeth

Skull of a Triceratops showing its teeth and horns

Stegosaurus was a herbivore that lived during the Jurassic period in North America. It had bony plates on its back, and spines on its tail for protection. Stegosaurus was probably a very gentle creature. It depended on its armor plating, rather than speed, to escape **predators**.

Stegosaurus

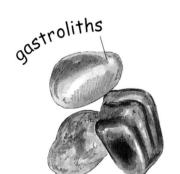

gastroliths

Stegosauruses, like many dinosaurs, swallowed stones to help their stomachs grind plant food to paste. These stones are called **gastroliths**.

Plateosaurus lived at the end of the Triassic period. It was one of the first large dinosaurs. It was about 23 feet (7 m) long and weighed 2 tons. The shape of its jaw and its rows of ridged teeth show that it was a herbivore. It might have been able to stand on its back legs and eat leaves that were out of reach of other dinosaurs.

Plateosaurus

Did Dinosaurs Eat Each Other?

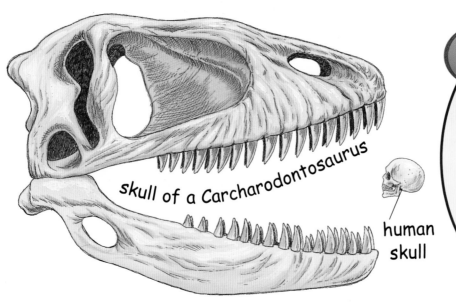

skull of a Carcharodontosaurus

human skull

Did You Know?

Carcharodontosaurus bones have been found in the Sahara desert. Its skull is 5 feet (1.6 m) long!

Carnivorous dinosaurs needed to eat meat to live. The best source of meat was other dinosaurs! Smaller dinosaurs may have caught lizards and insects. Others may have eaten fish.

All the meat-eaters had large, sharp, pointed teeth. However, they usually had fewer teeth than the herbivores.

The teeth of the Tyrannosaurus were up to 8 inches (20 cm) long. Only a small part of the tooth would have been seen above the gum line. Each tooth had an edge like a saw, which made it perfect for slicing through meat.

Tyrannosaurus

Megalosaurus was the first dinosaur to be named and was found in England in the early 1800s. Its teeth were perfect for a carnivore. They were long, sharp, and pointed backward. Dinosaurs grew new teeth throughout their life to replace broken and lost ones. Megalosaurus was about 30 feet (9 m) long.

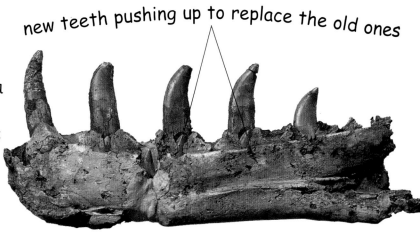

new teeth pushing up to replace the old ones

Part of a Megalosaurus jaw

Tyrannosaurus was 39 feet (12 m) long

Albertosaurus was 30 feet (9 m) long

Daspletosaurus was 30 feet (9 m) long

Did Dinosaurs Lay Eggs?

The first dinosaur eggs ever found were discovered in Mongolia in 1923. They are about the size of large potatoes and are believed to be from the small dinosaur called Protoceratops. Many more dinosaur eggs have been found since then. Since most reptiles lay eggs, scientists think that most dinosaurs laid eggs too.

Dinosaur nesting colony

Fossilized dinosaur nests full of eggs have been found in Mongolia and Canada. Most nests were dug into the ground and might have been lined with soft vegetation. Many have been found together in **nesting colonies**.

Fossilized dinosaur eggs

Dinosaur eggs can be different shapes. Some are long and oval, others are almost perfectly round. In some eggs, the fossils of the tiny, baby dinosaurs have also been found.

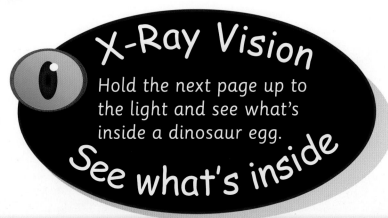

X-Ray Vision

Hold the next page up to the light and see what's inside a dinosaur egg.

See what's inside

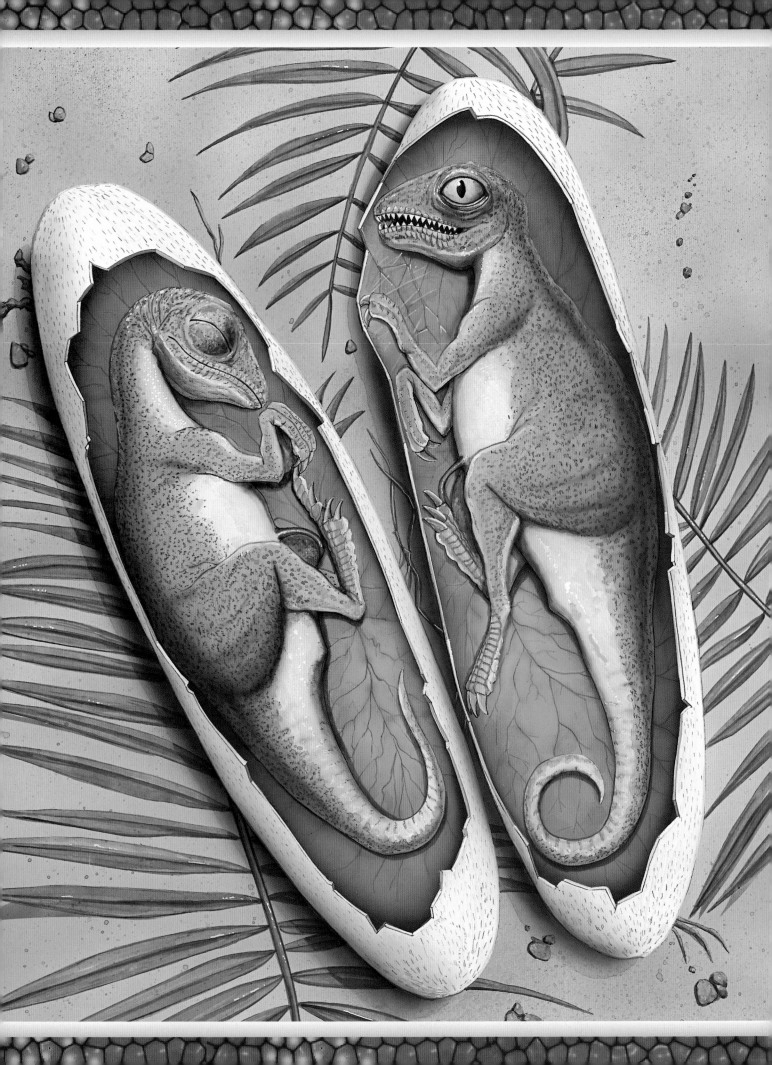

Were Dinosaurs Good Parents?

Newly hatched dinosaurs were tiny compared to their parents. The bones of some baby dinosaurs were too weak to support them at first. The parents must have protected them until they were strong enough to leave the nest. Other types of baby dinosaurs probably hatched ready to leave the nest right away.

Maiasaura parent feeding its young

Skeletons of baby Maiasaura dinosaurs have been found in nests in Montana. Their teeth were worn down. This could mean that their parents fed them while they were still in the nest.

The Maiasaura nests found in Montana were about 23 feet (7 m) apart from each other. This was about the same length as an adult. Each parent sitting on a nest was just far enough away from its neighbors that egg-stealing animals could not easily attack the nests.

Maiasaura young hatching

How Big Were Dinosaurs?

Dinosaurs were the biggest land-living animals on Earth. The biggest of all were a group of dinosaurs called the sauropods. Sauropod skeletons have been found all over the world. They were huge, four-legged plant-eaters with small heads, massive bodies, and long necks and tails. The best known are Brachiosaurus, Apatosaurus, and Diplodocus.

This skeleton of a Shunosaurus was found in China. It lived there about 160 million years ago. It was almost 33 feet (10 m) long and 10 feet (3 m) tall. Shunosaurus had only 12 **vertebrae** in its neck. Later sauropods had longer necks and longer tails.

Shunosaurus

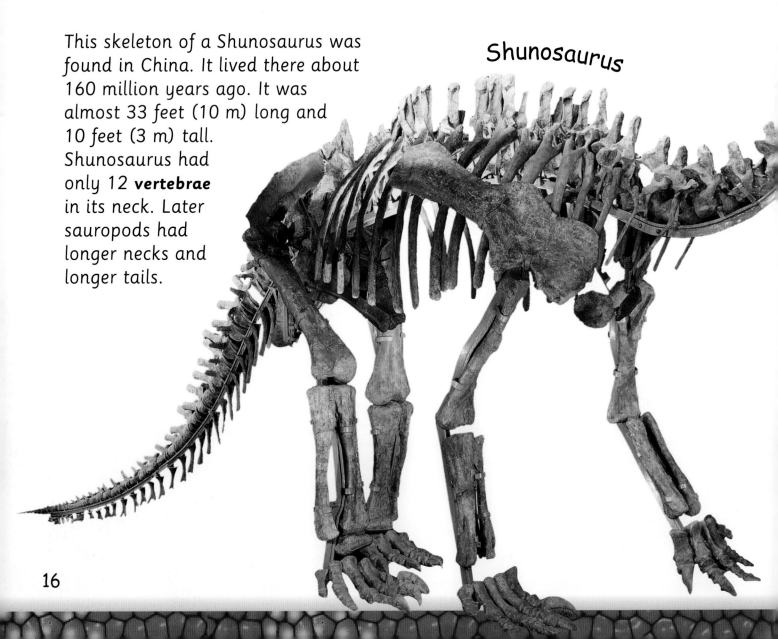

Mamenchisaurus had the longest neck of all the dinosaurs. It had 19 vertebrae. Mamenchisaurus might have used its neck to feed on the ground in wide arcs, without having to move its body.

Did You Know?

Brachiosaurus is the largest dinosaur for which a complete skeleton has been found. It was 82 feet (25 m) long, 39 feet (12 m) high, and weighed 50 tons!

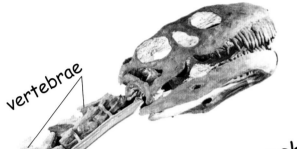

vertebrae

Mamenchisaurus

Modern-day elephant

Although dinosaurs were very large animals, they had small brains. The herbivorous dinosaurs, who probably relied on their size or armor plating for protection, had very small brains. The stegosaurs such as Stegosaurus, Kentrosaurus, and Huayangosaurus had the smallest brains of all. Their brains were about the size of a walnut!

The largest brains belonged to the huge carnivorous dinosaurs such as Albertosaurus. It had good eyesight and was a fast hunter.

Stegosaurus

Did Dinosaurs Live in Water?

Dinosaurs **evolved** to live on land. They did not live in the water, although they probably enjoyed cooling off in a river or lake. There were other reptiles that could only live in the water that lived at the same time as the dinosaurs. These included the plesiosaurs and ichthyosaurs.

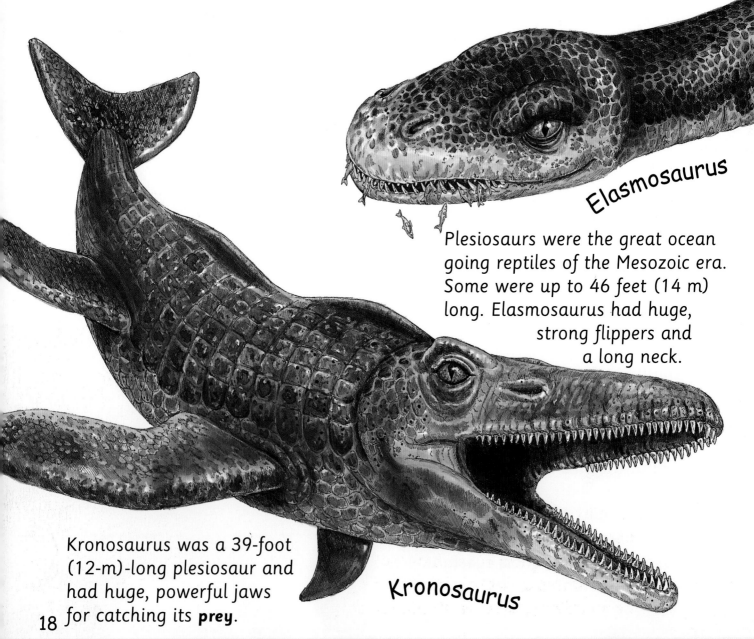

Elasmosaurus

Plesiosaurs were the great ocean going reptiles of the Mesozoic era. Some were up to 46 feet (14 m) long. Elasmosaurus had huge, strong flippers and a long neck.

Kronosaurus was a 39-foot (12-m)-long plesiosaur and had huge, powerful jaws for catching its **prey**.

Kronosaurus

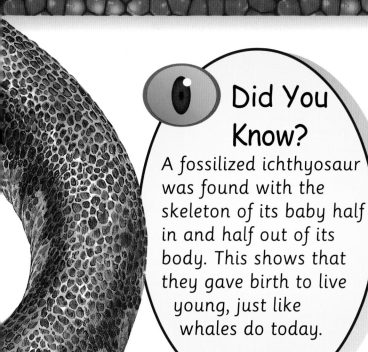

The ichthyosaurs were the dolphins and porpoises of the Mesozoic era. They were well adapted for swimming fast and hunting fish. They had powerful tails, streamlined bodies, and huge eyes. The earliest ichthyosaurs lived around 200 million years ago and survived right to the end of the Cretaceous period. That is when the dinosaurs also became extinct.

Ichthyosaurus lived in waters near Europe and North America during the Jurassic and Cretaceous periods. Hundreds of complete fossils have been found. Only 7 feet (2 m) long, it had powerful front paddles for steering and a large tail.

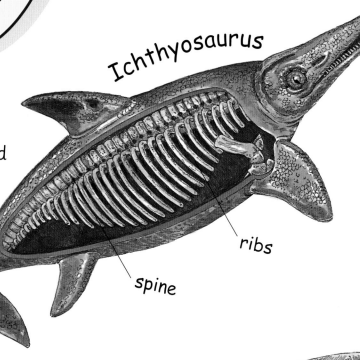

Ichthyosaurus

ribs

spine

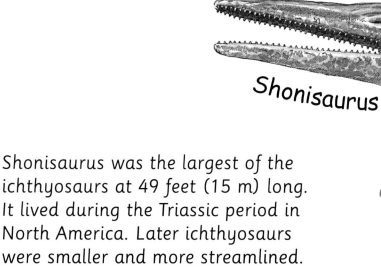

Shonisaurus

Shonisaurus was the largest of the ichthyosaurs at 49 feet (15 m) long. It lived during the Triassic period in North America. Later ichthyosaurs were smaller and more streamlined.

Did Dinosaurs Fly?

None of the dinosaurs could fly. The first group of backboned animals that learned to fly was the pterosaurs. These reptiles flew with wings made of skin. They first appear as fossils from late in the Triassic period, about 230 million years ago. The first birds appeared in the Jurassic period. Scientists believe that birds evolved from early forms of feathered dinosaurs.

bony crest

Pteranodon

Pteranodon was one of the larger pterosaurs. Its fossils have been found in Europe and North America. It had a short body, no tail, and a bony crest on its head. No one knows what the crest was for. Pteranodon probably glided over the oceans.

wings of skin

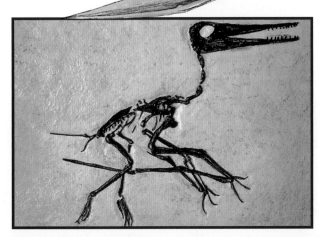

Pterodactylus was a small pterosaur common in Europe and Africa. There were many different types, but none of them had a **wingspan** of more than 30 inches (75 cm). Pterodactylus kochi had long narrow jaws with many sharp teeth. It probably skimmed over the sea and caught small fish with its open jaws.

Fossilized Pterodactylus kochi

Did dinosaurs have feathers?

Newly discovered fossils from China show that some small, early dinosaurs were covered in feathers. These creatures did not have wings and they were not birds. The feathers possibly evolved to keep the animals warm. These small, meat-eating dinosaurs had hollow bones so that they weighed less. Hollow bones were perfect for running fast and for early attempts at flying! Many scientists now think of birds as modern dinosaurs.

Yes, some dinosaurs had feathers.

Quetzalcoatlus

Archaeopteryx

The earliest known bird is called Archaeopteryx.
It was discovered in Germany in 1860.
It lived in the Jurassic period, about 160 million years ago.

Remains of several Archaeopteryx have been found, including some single feathers. Its skeleton is almost identical to a small, carnivorous dinosaur called Compsognathus. Only the feathers prove that it was a bird.

21

Albertosaurus

Large carnivores like Albertosaurus could probably run quickly for short distances. They could have reached speeds up to 25 mph (40 kph).

How Fast Were Dinosaurs?

Corythosaurus

Scientists study dinosaur skeletons to figure out their walking and running speeds. The distance between footprints left by running dinosaurs can be measured to show their speed. Carnivores could catch prey by running fast. Herbivores could escape them by trying to run even faster!

Duck-billed dinosaurs such as the Corythosaurus had three-toed feet ending in hooves. Though good for walking, these feet were probably too big for running very far. Corythosaurus probably lived in large herds to keep safe from predators!

The feet of large sauropods were perfect for supporting their weight but not for running. The sauropods' size and powerful tail was enough to scare off most attackers.

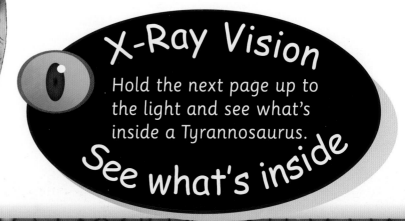

X-Ray Vision

Hold the next page up to the light and see what's inside a Tyrannosaurus.

See what's inside

Tyrannosaurus

skull

sharp teeth

ribs

vertebrae

thigh bone

claws

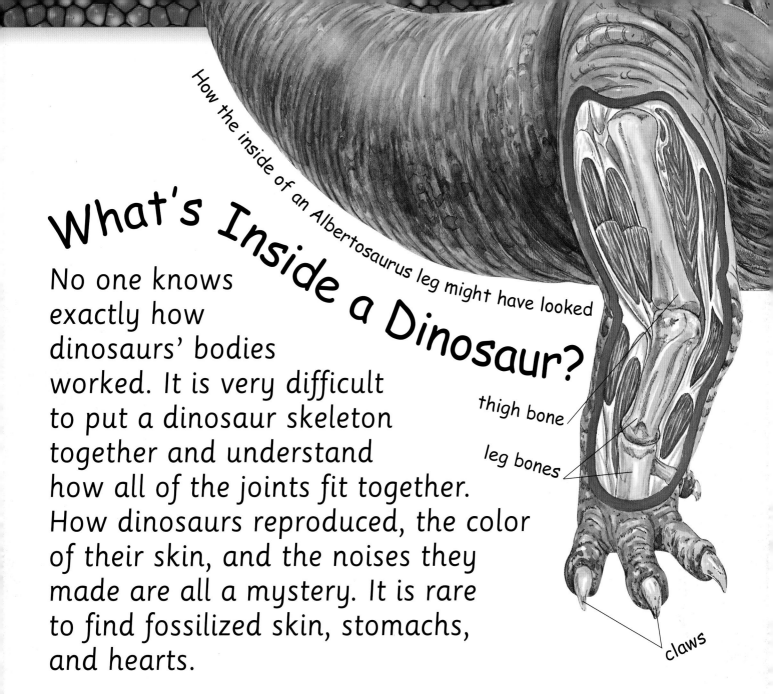

What's Inside a Dinosaur?

No one knows exactly how dinosaurs' bodies worked. It is very difficult to put a dinosaur skeleton together and understand how all of the joints fit together. How dinosaurs reproduced, the color of their skin, and the noises they made are all a mystery. It is rare to find fossilized skin, stomachs, and hearts.

thigh bone

leg bones

claws

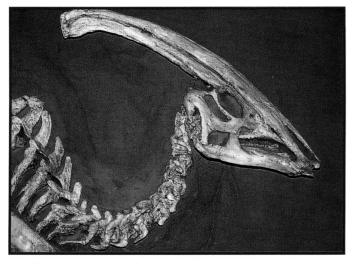

Fossilized Parasaurolophus skeleton

Dinosaur fossils are almost always the remains of hard body parts such as bones, teeth, eggshells, and gastroliths. It is very rare to find fossils of soft body parts because they rot away. Scientists use their knowledge of modern reptiles to figure out what the muscles and internal organs of dinosaurs were like.

How Do We Know About Dinosaurs?

Everything that we know about dinosaurs came from fossils discovered within the last 200 years. When bones are found, they have to be carefully dug up. Then they are taken to museums where scientists slowly remove the rock from around them using hammers, chisels, and other instruments.

Did You Know?

A complete Tyrannosaurus skeleton, dug up in South Dakota, was sold in 1997 for 8.4 million dollars! The dinosaur was thought to be female so it was named Sue, after the person who discovered it.

Dinosaur fossils are found in rocks all over the world. These two scientists (left) are working on the bones of a sauropod dinosaur. It is being **excavated** in the Sahara desert in Africa. They are strengthening weak areas of the bone with plaster.

Scientists excavating a dinosaur fossil

Fossils: from earth to museum

A fossilized bone is found and exposed by scraping away the rock around it.

As the bone dries in the air, it may need to be painted with resin to protect the surface.

The exposed bone is covered with plaster. The plaster hardens and protects the bone.

The bone is removed from the ground, and the rest of it is covered in plaster.

When the bones have been identified, artists illustrate how they might fit together.

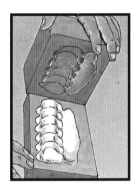

Rubber molds are made of the bones. Then the molds are used to make copies of the bones.

The copies are painted to match the original bones and the originals are safely stored.

The final stages might involve mounting the bones on a steel frame. Most modern dinosaur skeletons on display are made from lightweight copies of real bones. These are much easier to handle and not as fragile, or valuable. This scientist (right) is applying the finishing touches to a Massospondylus skeleton found in southern Africa.

Mounting a skeleton in a laboratory

What Happened to the Dinosaurs?

Sixty-five million years ago, something happened to Earth. Scientists believe that a huge asteroid hit the planet, plunging into the sea near the coast of Mexico. Scientists have found a crater beneath the seabed 112 miles (180 km) wide. The asteroid is estimated to have been 6 miles (10 km) wide and hit Earth at a speed of 62,000 mph (100,000 kph).

This impact would have caused dust in the atmosphere, volcanoes and earthquakes, enormous tidal waves, strong winds, and storms.

The skies became full of dust. Soon, the sun would disappear from view for many months. It would become very cold. Most plants, which normally need sunshine to live, would die.

The plant-eating dinosaurs would soon begin to suffer from the lack of food. In a few weeks they would begin to starve and die. Smaller reptiles, small mammals, and insects might survive because they need less food.

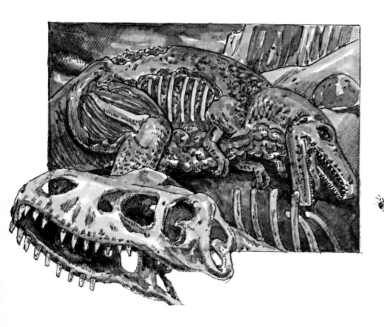

The carnivorous dinosaurs might feast on dead and dying herbivores, but once they were all gone, the carnivores would die too. Soon many types of animals, including all the dinosaurs, would be dead.

When the dust cleared, sunlight would reappear. Tiny animals such as earthworms, shrews, and insects would have survived by **scavenging**. Bigger animals, including crocodiles, snakes, and frogs, would come out of hibernation. Seeds buried in the ground would grow, and slowly the world would return to normal, but without the dinosaurs.

Dinosaur Facts

Scientists have studied fossilized dinosaur droppings discovered in Montana. The droppings contain a lot of wood fibers from trees. It appears that some herbivorous dinosaurs could eat very tough wood.

In one dinosaur nesting colony that has been found, 19 eggs were carefully arranged in a spiral inside the nests. Each nest had been dug into the ground.

Argentinosaurus is only known from the few leg bones and vertebrae that have been found. It was much bigger than any other dinosaur, perhaps up to 131 feet (40 m) long!

The largest known carnivorous dinosaur is Giganotosaurus found in Argentina. It was 52 feet (16 m) long and weighed more than 8 tons.

Skeletons of small carnivorous dinosaurs called Coelophysis were found in New Mexico. They were discovered to have the skeletons of young Coelophysis inside of their bodies. Coelophysis were cannibals!

When scientists carefully studied a number of different carnivorous dinosaurs, they discovered that about a quarter of the animals had fractures to their hands and feet. These may have happened when attacking other dinosaurs for food. Though probably painful for a while, such fractures would usually have healed themselves eventually.

A nest of eggs was found in Mongolia with a skeleton of a dinosaur called Oviraptor. It was once thought that Oviraptor was stealing and eating the eggs. Now scientists think that the Oviraptor died in a sandstorm while sitting on the nest trying to protect its own eggs.

Baryonyx was the first fish-eating dinosaur discovered. Its remains were found in Surrey, England in 1983 with the fossils of fish left in its stomach. Baryonyx had long jaws like a crocodile and huge claws to help it catch its prey.

Glossary

aggressive Something which shows fierceness.

carnivore Any animal that eats the flesh of other animals as its main food source.

Cretaceous The period of time that began about 135 million years ago and ended about 65 million years ago.

evolve To change in some way over a very long period of time.

excavate To find buried objects by digging them up.

extinct Species of animals that are no longer alive anywhere in the world.

fossil The very old remains of a plant or animal.

gastrolith A stone or pebble swallowed by an animal and kept in its stomach. Gastroliths help to grind up tough food.

herbivore Any animal that eats plant material as its main food source.

Jurassic The period of time that began about 208 million years ago and ended about 135 million years ago.

nesting colony An area where lots of the same type of animal make nests and have young.

predator An animal that hunts other living creatures for food.

prey Animals that are hunted by other animals for food.

reptile A cold-blooded animal that breathes with lungs.

scavenging Feeding on dead or rotting plants and animals.

Triassic The period of time that began about 245 million years ago and ended about 208 million years ago.

vertebrae The bones that fit together to form an animal's spine.

wingspan The distance measured between the wing tips of a bird.

Index